# GRIDDLE SIZZLE AND SEAR

# GRIDDLE SIZZLE AND SEAR

### Jenni Fleetwood

LORENZ BOOKS

This edition is published by Lorenz Books

Lorenz Books is an imprint of Anness Publishing Ltd
Hermes House, 88–89 Blackfriars Road, London SE1 8HA
tel. 020 7401 2077; fax 020 7633 9499
www.lorenzbooks.com; info@anness.com

© Anness Publishing Ltd 2004

UK agent: The Manning Partnership Ltd, tel. 01225 478 444;
fax 01225 478 440; sales@manning-partnership.co.uk

UK distributor: Grantham Book Services Ltd,
tel. 01476 541 080; fax 01476 541 061; orders@gbs.tbs-ltd.co.uk

North American agent/distributor: National Book Network,
tel. 301 459 3366; fax 301 429 5746; www.nbnbooks.com

Australian agent/distributor: Pan Macmillan Australia, tel. 1300 135 113; fax
1300 135 103; customer.service@macmillan.com.au

New Zealand agent/distributor: David Bateman Ltd,
tel. (09) 415 7664; fax (09) 415 8892

A CIP catalogue record for this book is available from the British Library.

PUBLISHER: Joanna Lorenz
MANAGING EDITOR: Helen Sudell
EXECUTIVE EDITOR: Joanne Rippin
PHOTOGRAPHERS: Martin Brigdale, William Lingwood, Don Last, Nick Dowey,
Sam Stowell.
RECIPES DEVISED BY: Rena Salaman, Kate Whiteman, Christine France, Brian
Glover, Marlena Spieler, Sallie Morris, Becky Johnson, Sally Mansfield.
DESIGNER: Adelle Morris
PRODUCTION CONTROLLER: Darren Price

10 9 8 7 6 5 4 3 2 1

NOTES
Bracketed terms are intended for American readers.

For all recipes, quantities are given in both metric and imperial measures
and, where appropriate, measures are also given in standard cups and
spoons. Follow one set, but not a mixture, because they are not
interchangeable.

Standard spoon and cup measures are level.
1 tsp = 5ml, 1 tbsp = 15ml, 1 cup = 250ml/8fl oz

Australian standard tablespoons are 20ml. Australian readers should use 3
tsp in place of 1 tbsp for measuring small quantities of gelatine, salt, etc.

Medium (US large) eggs are used unless otherwise stated.

# CONTENTS

# INTRODUCTION

The aroma of food grilling on the barbecue or griddle is irresistible. There's something about this style of cooking that appeals to everyone, from children hankering for hot dogs to stylish sophisticates tucking into peppery monkfish. What was once an occasional pastime is rapidly becoming a regular occurrence, and the good news is that you don't have to go into the garden to experience the great flavour of grilled food. Invest in a good griddle and you can enjoy indoors what is conventionally cooked over the coals.

If you do take the griddle outside, however, you double the pleasure. Cooking and eating in the open air is hugely enjoyable, and just as we like making our gardens into extensions of our home, it's good to take our everyday activities out there too. With the vast array of equipment dedicated to the outdoor cook, preparing food outside can be as simple or as sophisticated as you want it to be. Built-in, brick barbecues have been overtaken by gas appliances that rival modern ranges, with rotisseries, warming racks, hoods and a host of other refinements. Solar lights, candles and flickering torches illuminate the garden and add to the atmosphere, portable refrigerators cool the drinks, and heaters take the chill off cooler evenings.

As national cuisines become more and more infused with other cultural influences, griddled food is also becoming more diverse and imaginative. Different ingredients, flavourings and methods are added to a traditional repertoire, and the result is a diversity of styles and tastes. Once the preserve of meat and fish-eaters only, in some cultures, barbecues now also cater much more for vegetarians, with delicious, well-flavoured alternatives to the traditional burger or steak. There's even an array of sweet treats to finish off the grilling event. Dishes like baked bananas with vanilla ice cream, grilled nectarines with marzipan and mascarpone and pineapple wedges with a rum glaze are easy to cook and delicious to eat.

With dishes that reflect the diversity that is available, featuring recipes from around the world, and using ingredients that will expand your repertoire and tantalize your tastebuds, this little book holds an astonishing array of griddling, sizzling and searing ideas.

# SUCCESSFUL GRIDDLING

Before you begin using the barbecue or grill, make sure you are properly prepared. This chapter contains vital information, hints and tips for perfect griddling results.

# BARBECUE EQUIPMENT

When it comes to equipping an outside cooking area, there's almost as much equipment available as there is for the kitchen indoors. From long-handled matches to flashy appliances that do everything except serve the food, the choice is dazzling.

## BARBECUES

Which type of barbecue to buy depends on a host of factors, including the space available, the amount of money you have to spend and your personal style of cooking. If the ritual is what matters, and you love the whole operation of building the fire and judging just when the coals are perfect for grilling, a charcoal barbecue – still the most popular type – will be ideal. If you go in for impromptu entertaining, when speed and efficiency are prime considerations, you'll probably opt for a gas model.

Whichever type of barbecue you choose, you'll extend its use if you also invest in a griddle. This can be a relatively small ridged pan, to be used outside or in the kitchen, or a much larger utensil designed to fit over your existing barbecue, converting the entire cooking area to one which heats evenly. A griddle simplifies the cooking of small items, or fragile ones such as fish, which might otherwise fall through the gaps in the grid.

**charcoal barbecues** There are several different types of charcoal barbecue. The hibachi is basically a firebox on legs, with a tray in the base to hold the coals. There are several rungs for the grill rack, so its height can be varied, depending on the degree of heat required for cooking. Although described as portable, this type of barbecue is fairly heavy, so for beach parties and

BELOW: A hibachi barbecue. A simple, straightforward design.

BELOW: The enduringly popular kettle barbecue complete with lid.

ABOVE: **Instant barbecues can be made with stones or bricks.**

similar events, a disposable barbecue is more convenient.

This can be placed on the ground, or on a table, in which case it is important to insulate the surface by using a separate stand. Disposable barbecues are very easy to use – you simply light the fuel-soaked pad that ignites the coals, then place the food on the mesh cover – but the heat

cannot be controlled. Unless you keep the food constantly on the move, burnt offerings are a very real risk.

Another type of charcoal grill is the brazier. This also has an open firebox, and may include a motor-driven spit or rotisserie. This type of barbecue often has a windbreak at the back, which is helpful when you are trying to get the fire started, especially as there are seldom any vents in the base to help to improve the air flow to the coals. The cast-iron pot-bellied or barrel

brazier stands on short legs and has a sliding grate in the base for removing the ash easily. Air vents speed up the burning process, so the coals are ready to use in 30 minutes. The grill rack can be adjusted to several heights, but this type of barbecue does not usually have a lid. Improvise with tented heavy-duty foil.

The most popular category of charcoal barbecue is the kettle. This stands on legs and looks rather like a large orange that has been cut in

LEFT: A griddle can be placed on top of a barbecue, as well as used inside on a gas or electric stove.

**gas barbecues** Efficient and easy to use, these represent the most rapidly growing sector of the barbecue market. Initially dismissed by many as failing to provide the authentic barbecue flavour, they now give very good results, thanks to "hot rocks" or angled metal bars which instantly vaporize the cooking juices that drip on to them, so that the steam rises to flavour the food above.

Modern gas barbecues tend to be used in much the same way as a kitchen stove. Both are equally simple to switch on, take about the same time – 15 minutes or so – to reach cooking temperature, and give reliable results. Small wonder that gas barbecues have become highly desirable objects, with luxury models incorporating all kinds of additions and gimmicks, including stainless steel grates, weather-resistant work surfaces, rotisseries and even built-in smoker systems. If you have several burners, you will probably be able to vary the temperature on different parts of the grill.

half across the equator. The fire is made on a grid in the base. Adjustable vents encourage it to burn efficiently and when the coals reach cooking temperature a large circular grill is set on top. The entire top half of the barbecue consists of a domed lid, also vented, which extends the versatility of the appliance. As well as being ideal for chops, chicken portions, sausages, vegetable slices, fish steaks and other small items,

it can be used for cooking whole chickens or joints of meat. For these, the coals are raked aside and a drip tray placed under the food. The lid and the base reflect the heat evenly, so the food develops an all-round golden tan and is cooked evenly, as on a rotisserie.

Modern kettle barbecues can be fitted with various accessories, including a large wok that fits inside the base, perfect for *al fresco* stir-fries.

## GRIDDLES

These are sold in various sizes and designs, and are invaluable for both indoor and outdoor grilling. The smaller, portable griddles look like square ridged frying pans. The best ones are made entirely of cast iron, although some are cast iron with a hinged metal handle. Griddles can be used on the hob, on the barbecue or in the oven, providing a solid surface which, when very hot, will sear food and seal in the cooking juices.

Built-in ridged griddles are a feature of some of the more sophisticated kitchen stoves. Seated snugly over a burner in the centre of the hob, the griddle heats along its length, giving a large cooking area.

Get used to thinking of your griddle as an adjunct to your barbecue, as well as an invaluable kitchen utensil.

## SAFETY TIPS

Cooking on a barbecue is safe if it's done sensibly – use these simple guidelines as a checklist to safeguard against accidents. If you have never organized a barbecue before, keep your first few events as simple as possible.

• Make sure the barbecue is sited on a firm and level surface. Once it is lit, do not move it.
• Never pour flammable liquid on to a lit barbecue.
• Keep children and pets well away from the fire, and always make sure the cooking is supervised by adults.
• Keep perishable foods cold until you are ready to cook, especially in hot weather. Make sure meat, especially pork and chicken, is thoroughly cooked. If you start chicken off in a microwave before finishing off on the barbecue, don't allow the meat to

BELOW: **Covering food with foil will keep moisture locked in.**

cool down in between. Never reheat poultry once it has cooled.
• Keep raw food away from cooked. Wash your hands after handling raw meat and before touching anything else. Don't use the same utensils for raw ingredients and cooked food.
• Use long-handled tools, such as forks, tongs and brushes, for turning and basting food; keep some oven gloves handy, preferably the extra-long type to protect your hands.
• Have a bucket of sand and a water spray on hand to douse any flames that get out of control.

BELOW: **Always use long-handled barbecue tools.**

# COOKING TIPS AND TECHNIQUES

The old adage about practice making perfect could have been written for barbecue cooks. It has most relevance for those cooking over wood or charcoal, but even those grilling on gas will need time to get used to the vagaries of their individual appliances.

Whatever type of barbecue you own, it is vital to familiarize yourself with the operating instructions in the handbook. Owners of gas appliances should check that all the gas fittings and the hose attachments are tight before lighting in the right manner.

A charcoal barbecue is a bit more demanding. Lay the fire in good time, bearing in mind that once you light it, it will be at least 30 minutes before the coals are ready. A couple of layers of lumpwood charcoal or a packed, single layer of briquettes on the fuel rack should give you sufficient heat to run a barbecue for 1–1½ hours.

Lumpwood charcoal works well in an open brazier, but if you are building the fire on a grid, use briquettes as they won't fall through the bars.

The most efficient shape for a barbecue fire is the pyramid. As kindling use spills of newspaper or dried hardwood twigs from fruit trees such as apple, pear or plum.

Woody herb branches, like rosemary, bay or thyme, also work well. Heap the charcoal over the kindling. Lumpwood charcoal ignites quickly if used in this manner, but briquettes, which are harder to ignite, may need a little encouragement. Tuck one or two firelighters into the pyramid.

An easy and safe way to get the fire going in a kettle barbecue is to use a fire chimney. This is a broad metal cylinder with air holes punched in the sides. It is placed upright on the fire grid. Newspaper is placed in the base and the space above is filled with

BELOW: **A fire chimney keeps the charcoal piled together until ready.**

briquettes. When the newspaper is lit, it ignites the bottom layer of fuel. As the charcoal burns, it ignites each layer above it until the top coals are dusted with ash. The entire process takes about half an hour. At this stage, the chimney can be lifted off carefully and the coals spread.

As the coals burn the temperature drops to medium, and the ash covering gets slightly thicker, with only dots of red showing through. This is good for most foods. When the ash is very thick and the coals are on the verge of collapse, the heat will be low.

## USING THE HEAT WISELY

By piling the coals up in the centre of the firebox, you can create a central hot spot surrounded by cooler areas. Items that can cope with high temperatures can be started off in the middle and then moved to the sides. The hot spot can also be used for rustling up a quickly cooked first course, such as marinated prawns (shrimp) or toasted slices of ciabatta topped with a rich tomato sauce.

When the coals cool a little, you can cook items that need a little more time, like chicken portions or lamb kebabs. Again, watch the heat closely,

ABOVE: **Cook fish and shellfish first while the heat is high.**
LEFT: **Marinating meat first will keep it tender and add flavour.**

and move items to the outer rim if they seem to be cooking too quickly. Some cuts of chicken, like quarters or thighs, are surprisingly dense. It is vital that the meat is cooked right through to the bone, so always check before serving. If you are nervous about cooking chicken, start the pieces off in the microwave. Arrange portions with the thinnest pieces towards the centre and cook for about 10 minutes on maximum power before transferring to the grill.

Fish, chicken breasts and most vegetables need medium to low heat. Wait until the coals have an even dusting of ash, or raise the barbecue grill. Spreading the coals lowers the temperature; bunching them raises it.

After you have served the main course, there will still be a lot of heat left in the fire. Use this to cook desserts like baked bananas. Put whole bananas on the grill until their skins turn evenly black. Slit, peel and serve with ice cream.

### COOKING ON A GRIDDLE

Whether you are using a griddle on top of a barbecue, or inside on a stove, the following applies. It is very important that the griddle is searing hot and very dry when the food is first put on to it. A few drops of water shaken on to the surface should evaporate instantly. Oil the food, not the griddle, and, to help reduce the amount of smoke, pat off any excess marinade with kitchen paper. As soon as the food is seared, lower the heat.

# TASTES AND FLAVOURS

Wherever the weather is warm enough for cooking out of doors, grill and griddle recipes have been developed. This is great news for the modern grill cook, since it provides the opportunity to try exciting flavour combinations that are a world away from bland burgers or pallid pieces of chicken. The recipes in this book come from Greece, France, Thailand, Malaysia, Morocco and the United States. Although the dishes vary widely in terms of flavour, the cooking method imposes certain universal criteria on the basic ingredients – top quality, tenderness and good taste.

## QUALITY INGREDIENTS

Grilling is such a rapid form of cooking that it does not suffer the second-rate. Tough meat will stay that way, and stringy vegetables will not soften, so it is essential to use only the best ingredients for the barbecue or griddle. Buy from an organic supplier where possible, and opt for fresh rather than frozen foods. This is especially important as regards shellfish, which can become dry and tasteless on thawing.

Buy your meat from a reputable local supplier, getting to know your

ABOVE: **Use fresh rather than pre-served spices for authentic flavour.**

butcher so that he can advise you on the best cuts for grilling. Some butchers make their own kebabs as well as coils of boerewors and other specialist sausages, which can be useful additions to your menu.

Fish cooks beautifully on the barbecue or griddle. Mackerel, sardines, tuna and salmon are good choices, as their natural oils keep them beautifully moist, but red mullet, haddock, halibut, sea bass, snapper and turbot also cook very well. Choose thick fillets or steaks, and do not have the heat too high or the fish

ABOVE: **Bundles of aromatic twigs will scent the food and the air.**

will dry out. Swordfish is deservedly a favourite fish for grilling, especially when first marinated in olive oil and lemon juice.

Vegetable kebabs are enjoyed by everyone, but for an even simpler accompaniment, you can cook vegetable slices directly on the grill or griddle. Aubergines (eggplant) love this treatment and taste wonderful with a rich tomato topping. Cheese makes a good partner for vegetables, either as a filling for courgettes (zucchini) or with roasted onions. Some cheeses, such as Kefalotyri or Halloumi, are robust enough to retain their shape when grilled or griddled, and taste delicious with peppery rocket (arugula) or a simple radish and radicchio salad.

## HERBS, SPICES AND SEASONINGS

If your kitchen is well stocked, preparing food for an impromptu barbecue will be much easier. Dried herbs and spices, such as thyme, marjoram, chilli powder, ground coriander and cumin are useful for rubs and marinades, and keep an eye out for more unusual items such as Australian aniseed myrtle, crushed pasilla chillies, Mexican oregano and ground sumac berries. Asia has contributed some wonderful recipes to grill cuisine, and for these you'll need fish sauce, oyster sauce, light and dark soy sauce and sesame oil, as well as a reliable supplier of fresh coriander (cilantro) and lemon grass.

## WRAPS AND BREADS

For a casual barbecue, it is great to be able to eat with your hands, using tortillas or pitta breads as vehicles for grilled food. Crisp the wraps over the heat first, if you like. Ciabatta and other speciality breads, onion rolls and

RIGHT: **Toasted ciabatta is perfect with fresh tomatoes and olive oil.**

baps for burgers are so useful that it is worth keeping a supply in the freezer. For a simple snack, toast slices of ciabatta on the grill and top with warm chopped tomatoes and olives in oil.

## INSTANT APPETIZERS

Fires can be fickle, so you need to be flexible when planning a meal cooked on the grill or griddle. Keep hunger at bay with simple nibbles like hand-made crisps (US potato chips) with a couple of dips. Cream cheese mixed with finely chopped spring onions (scallions) and parsley is delicious, as is a mixture of crumbled blue cheese, soft cheese and Greek (US strained plain) yogurt. Or mix a carton of sour cream with a tablespoon of ready-made red or green pesto. This tastes great with crisp crudités or grilled Mediterranean vegetables.

Even easier are individual shallow bowls of virgin olive oil served with bread dippers. The olive oil can be as nature intended, beaded with balsamic vinegar or flavoured with chopped fresh herbs and crushed garlic. For an unusual dip, stir *zahtar*, a slightly

sweet thyme-flavoured spice blend from the Middle East, into olive oil. Other quick and easy appetizers include selections of black olives, smoked oysters, caperberries and sun-dried tomatoes in oil. Baby radishes, dipped in softened butter and then in salt, make the classic French nibble, *radis au beurre*.

# RUBS AND MARINADES

One of the best ways of flavouring meat, poultry or fish is by using an aromatic spice mixture. This can either be rubbed in before cooking, or mixed with liquid to make a marinade.

## PHILADELPHIA RUB

This makes a great seasoning for pork steaks or chops. Rub it into the meat at least 1 hour before grilling.

MAKES ABOUT 45ML/3 TBSP

8 cloves
2.5ml/$^1$/$_2$ tsp grated nutmeg
1.5ml/$^1$/$_4$ tsp ground mace
5ml/1 tsp dried basil
5ml/1 tsp dried thyme
2 dried bay leaves
salt

**1** Using a mortar and pestle or spice mill, grind the cloves to a coarse powder, then add the nutmeg, mace and dried herbs. Continue grinding the mixture until fine.
**2** Rub into the meat and leave to stand before placing it on the grill.

## CAJUN SPICE MIX

This classic mixture is marvellous on fish steaks, chicken or meat.

MAKES ABOUT 150ML/$^1$/$_4$ PINT/$^2$/$_3$ CUP

5ml/1 tsp black peppercorns
5ml/1 tsp cumin seeds

ABOVE: **Rubs are a quick way of adding flavour to meat.**

5ml/1 tsp white mustard seeds
10ml/2 tsp paprika
5ml/1 tsp chilli powder or
   cayenne pepper
5ml/1 tsp dried oregano
5ml/1 tsp dried thyme
5ml/1 tsp salt
2 garlic cloves
1 onion, sliced

**1** Dry-fry the peppercorns, cumin seeds and mustard seeds over a medium heat for 3–4 minutes.
**2** Put into a mortar or spice mill and grind to powder. Add the paprika, chilli powder or cayenne pepper, oregano, thyme and salt. Grind again.

**3** Transfer the mixture to a blender or food processor (using the mini bowl if you have one) and add the garlic and onion. Process the mixture until thoroughly combined.
**4** Press the spice mix into the portions of fish, chicken or meat and leave to stand for 1–2 hours so that the flavours are absorbed.

## DEEP HEAT

A variation on the classic barbecue spice, this rub works well with all types of meats. Leave it to stand for 30 minutes before grilling.

MAKES ABOUT 60ML/4 TBSP

10ml/2 tsp celery seeds
5ml/1 tsp crushed dried red chillies
5ml/1 tsp paprika
5ml/1 tsp grated nutmeg
5ml/1 tsp garlic powder
5ml/1 tsp onion salt
10ml/2 tsp dried marjoram
5ml/1 tsp salt
5–10ml/1–2 tsp brown sugar
5ml/1 tsp ground black pepper

**1** In a spice mill or mortar, grind the celery seeds to a powder.
**2** Stir in the all the remaining ingredients and use the rub immediately or store in an airtight container in a cool, dark place.

## JUNIPER SPICE BLEND

This pungent mixture is great on duck breasts and beef. With ostrich and venison, it works best as a marinade, adding the moisture that can be lacking in low-fat meats.

MAKES ABOUT 60ML/4 TBSP

30ml/2 tbsp juniper berries
5ml/1 tsp black peppercorns
2.5ml/¹/₂ tsp sea salt
5ml/1 tsp ground allspice
15ml/1 tbsp soft dark brown sugar

FOR A MARINADE

120ml/4fl oz/¹/₂ cup gin
1-2 shallots, finely chopped
leaves from 2–3 fresh rosemary sprigs

**1** Using a mortar and pestle, or a spice mill, grind the juniper berries with the peppercorns and salt. Stir in the allspice and sugar.
**2** Rub the spice mixture on to all sides of meats before cooking them on the barbecue or griddle.
**3** To convert the spice mixture to a marinade, mix it with the gin, shallots and rosemary.
**4** Lay the pieces of meat in a single layer in a shallow dish, pour over the marinade and turn to coat.
**5** Cover and marinate, turning the pieces over occasionally, for 4–6 hours or overnight in the refrigerator.

ABOVE: **For a simple marinade, just add a bunch of fresh herbs, such as rosemary, to virgin olive oil.**

## HERB MARINADE

This simple mixture is good for fish, poultry and meat. Flavoured with thyme and oregano, it makes an excellent marinade for lamb cubes intended for kebabs.

MAKES ABOUT 200ML/7FL OZ/ SCANT 1 CUP

120ml/4fl oz/¹/₂ cup dry white wine
15ml/1 tbsp lemon juice
60ml/4 tbsp extra virgin olive oil
30ml/2 tbsp finely chopped fresh herbs, such as parsley, thyme, oregano, chives or basil
ground black pepper

**1** Put the wine and lemon juice in a bowl or jug (pitcher). Whisk in the olive oil, then stir in the herbs. Grind in a little black pepper.
**2** Lay the pieces of meat in a single layer in a shallow dish, pour over the marinade and turn to coat.
**3** Cover and marinate, turning the pieces over occasionally, for 4–6 hours or overnight in the refrigerator.

## RED WINE MARINADE

This is good with red meats and game, especially ostrich meat.

MAKES ABOUT 175ML/6FL OZ/³/₄ CUP

150ml/¹/₄ pint/²/₃ cup dry red wine
15ml/1 tbsp red wine vinegar
15ml/1 tbsp olive oil
2 garlic cloves, crushed
2 dried bay leaves, crumbled
ground black pepper

**1** Put the wine and vinegar in a bowl or jug (pitcher). Whisk in the olive oil, then stir in the crushed garlic and crumbled bay leaves. Add a little freshly ground black pepper.
**2** Lay the pieces of meat or game in a single layer in a shallow dish, pour over the marinade and turn to coat.
**3** Cover and marinate, turning the pieces over occasionally, for 4–6 hours or overnight in the refrigerator.

# GRILL AND GRIDDLE

Once you have assembled the equipment and mastered the arts of grilling, you are ready for the following delicious recipes for all occasions and palates.

# GRILLED SQUID WITH FETA AND MARJORAM

Succulent and full of flavour, these unusual barbecue treats come from Greece. The creamy cheese filling in the pouches contrasts beautifully with the portions that are chargrilled until crisp.

**INGREDIENTS**

SERVES 4

4 medium squid, total weight
    about 900g/2lb
4–8 finger-length slices of
    feta cheese
90ml/6 tbsp olive oil
2 garlic cloves, crushed
4 fresh marjoram sprigs,
    chopped
salt and ground black pepper
lemon wedges, to serve

**1** If using wooden skewers, soak them in cold water for 30 minutes.

**2** Rinse each squid well, then, holding the body firmly, pull away the head and tentacles. If the ink sac is still intact, remove and discard it.

**3** Pull out the innards, including the long transparent "pen", then peel off and discard the thin purple skin from the body, retaining the two side fins. Sever the tentacles. Squeeze the tentacles at the head end to push out the round beak in the centre. Throw this away. Rinse the prepared squid thoroughly and drain well.

**4** Place the squid in a single layer in a shallow dish. Tuck the pieces of feta between the squid.

**5** Make the marinade by whisking the oil, garlic and marjoram together in a jug (pitcher). Pour over the squid and cheese, cover and leave to marinate for 2–3 hours, turning the squid once.

**6** Insert 2 or 3 pieces of cheese and a few marjoram leaves from the marinade into each squid pouch. Thread the tentacles on skewers. Season the squid pouches and tentacles with salt and black pepper.

**7** Grill the stuffed squid on a barbecue or griddle over a fairly low heat for about 6 minutes, then turn them over carefully and cook for 1–2 minutes more.

**8** Add the skewered tentacles to the grill and cook for 2 minutes on each side, until they are slightly scorched. Serve with the lemon wedges.

# MARINATED RED MULLET WITH RASPBERRY DRESSING

This dish owes its fabulous flavour to fresh raspberries and raspberry vinegar.

## INGREDIENTS

SERVES 4

8 red mullet or small red
  snapper fillets
15ml/1 tbsp olive oil
15ml/1 tbsp raspberry vinegar
175g/6oz mixed salad leaves
salt and ground black pepper

FOR THE DRESSING

115g/4oz/1 cup raspberries,
  puréed and sieved
30ml/2 tbsp raspberry vinegar
60ml/4 tbsp extra virgin olive oil
1.5–2.5ml/$^1/_4$–$^1/_2$ tsp caster
  (superfine) sugar

**1** Lay the fillets in a shallow dish. Whisk together the oil and vinegar, add a pinch of salt and pour over the fish. Cover and leave to marinate for 30 minutes.

**2** In a salad bowl, whisk all the ingredients for the dressing together and season to taste. Set aside a third of the mixture and add the salad leaves to the remainder. Toss lightly to coat.

**3** Cook the fish fillets on a hot griddle or in a hinged grill over a medium heat for about 2–3 minutes on each side, until just cooked. Cut in half diagonally.

**4** Arrange a heap of dressed salad leaves on each plate. Prop up four pieces of fish on each and spoon the reserved dressing around. Serve immediately.

### COOK'S TIP

To purée the raspberries, whiz them in a blender or food processor, then press through a sieve to remove the seeds.

# MACKEREL AND RED ONION KEBABS

Oily fish like mackerel are great for grilling, as they stay moist.

**1** Soak 4 long wooden or bamboo skewers in water for 30 minutes to prevent them scorching.

**2** Make the marinade by whisking the oregano, wine, oil and lime juice together in a bowl.

**3** Drain the skewers and thread each one in and out through a mackerel fillet. Stick an onion wedge on either end. Place the skewers in a shallow dish and pour the marinade over. Cover and chill for 30 minutes, turning three or four times.

**4** Cook the kebabs on a barbecue or griddle over a medium heat for 10–12 minutes, occasionally turning the skewers and basting the fish with the marinade. Serve with lime wedges.

**COOK'S TIP**
If cooking indoors on a griddle, make sure the wooden skewers are not in contact with the surface. Pat the fish with kitchen paper before cooking to remove the excess oil and limit the amount of smoke produced.

**INGREDIENTS**

SERVES 4

30ml/2 tbsp chopped fresh
  oregano
60ml/4 tbsp dry white wine
45ml/3 tbsp olive oil
juice of 1 lime
4 mackerel, about 225g/8oz
  each, filleted
2 small red onions, cut
  in wedges
lime wedges, to serve

# PAPRIKA MONKFISH WITH CHORIZO AND PEPPERS

Monkfish is perfect for the barbecue or the griddle because it stays intact. It is also able to hold its own with very strong flavours, such as smoky paprika, charred peppers and spicy chorizo. These robust ingredients are cooled with a cucumber and mint sauce.

**1** Place both monkfish fillets in a flat dish. Rub them all over with salt, then cover and leave in a cool place. Pour the yogurt for the sauce into a food processor. Cut the cucumber into it, season with a little salt and pulse to a purée. Transfer to a serving bowl and stir in the mint.

**2** Rinse the salt off the fish and pat dry with kitchen paper. Rub the paprika evenly over the fish.

**3** Slice each pepper into twelve long strips and cut each fish fillet into ten equal pieces. Thread six pieces of pepper and five pieces of fish each onto four skewers and brush one side with olive oil.

**4** When the barbecue is ready, with medium hot coals, grill the kebabs oil side down for about 3–4 minutes. Brush the top side with oil, turn over and cook for another 3–4 minutes more.

**5** Remove the fish from the barbecue. Grill the chorizo slices for a second or two until warmed through. Thread one slice on to the end of each skewer and serve the rest alongside, with the cucumber and mint sauce.

### INGREDIENTS
SERVES 4

1 monkfish tail, about 1kg/2¼lb, trimmed and filleted
10ml/2 tsp smoked red paprika
2 red (bell) peppers, halved and seeded
15ml/1 tbsp extra virgin olive oil
16 thin slices of chorizo
salt and ground black pepper
FOR THE CUCUMBER AND MINT SAUCE
150ml/¼ pint/⅔ cup Greek (US strained plain) yoghurt
½ cucumber, halved lengthways and seeded
30ml/2 tbsp chopped fresh mint leaves

### VARIATION
Alternate the slices of pepper with red onion if you like

# GRIDDLED PRAWN AND MANGO SALAD WITH FRIZZLED SHALLOTS

Grilling is a favourite method of cooking in Thailand, where this delicious salad originated. The garlic and chilli dressing goes very well with both the seafood and the salad.

## INGREDIENTS

SERVES 4

675g/1¹/₂lb raw tiger prawns
    (jumbo shrimp), shelled
finely shredded rind of 1 lime
1 fresh red chilli, finely shredded
30ml/2 tbsp olive oil, plus extra
    for brushing
1 ripe but firm mango, peeled
2 carrots, cut into long
    thin shreds
10cm/4in piece
    cucumber, sliced
1 small red onion, halved and
    thinly sliced
a few sprigs each of fresh
    coriander (cilantro) and mint
45ml/3 tbsp roasted
    peanuts, chopped
4 large shallots, thinly sliced and
    fried until crisp
salt and ground black pepper

FOR THE DRESSING

1 large garlic clove, crushed
10ml/2 tsp caster
    (superfine) sugar
45ml–60ml/3–4 tbsp lime juice
15ml/1 tbsp Thai fish sauce
¹/₂ fresh red chilli, chopped
5ml/1 tsp light rice vinegar

**1** Mix the prawns, lime rind and half the chilli in a glass dish. Season, then spoon over the oil. Toss to mix, cover and marinate for 30 minutes.

**2** Make the dressing by whisking the ingredients in a jug (pitcher) or bowl.

**3** Cut the mango off the stone (pit) and slice it into long, thin strips. Place in a large bowl. Add the carrots, cucumber and onion slices to the mango, pour over half the dressing and mix lightly. Divide the mixture among four salad plates.

**4** Heat a griddle on the stove or the barbecue. When it is very hot, add the prawns and sear them for 2–3 minutes on each side, until they turn pink and are patched with brown.

**5** Arrange the prawns on the salad plates, sprinkle the remaining dressing over and place the herb sprigs on top. Sprinkle over the peanuts, crisp-fried shallots and remaining shredded chilli. Serve immediately.

# MOROCCAN GRILLED FISH BROCHETTES

If you can, use both a barbecue and a griddle to prepare these brochettes.

## INGREDIENTS

SERVES 4

5 garlic cloves, chopped
2.5ml/¹/₂ tsp paprika
2.5ml/¹/₂ tsp ground cumin
1.5ml/¹/₄ tsp cayenne pepper
2.5ml/¹/₂ tsp salt
60ml/4 tbsp olive oil
30ml/2 tbsp lemon juice
30ml/2 tbsp chopped fresh
    coriander (cilantro)
675g/¹/₂lb haddock or sea bass,
    in 2.5cm/1in cubes
2–3 green (bell) peppers
1 courgette (zucchini), sliced
1 red (bell) pepper, sliced

**1** If using wooden skewers, immerse them in cold water to soak. Meanwhile, mix the garlic, spices, salt, oil, lemon juice and coriander in a bowl. Add the fish and toss to coat. Cover and marinate for 30 minutes.

**2** Cut the green peppers into pieces. Remove the fish from the marinade. Thread the cubes alternately with the pepper pieces on the drained skewers.

**3** Grill the brochettes on a barbecue over a medium heat for 2–3 minutes on each side, until the fish is tender and very slightly browned.

**4** Meanwhile, cook the courgette and red pepper slices on a hot griddle until softened and lightly charred. Serve with the fish brochettes and lemon wedges.

### COOK'S TIP

If you prefer to cook the fish indoors on the griddle, cut it into four pieces rather than cubes. Marinate it as in the main recipe, but don't bother with the skewers.

# PEPPERED MONKFISH WITH CITRUS STUFFING

A delicious contrast between flakes of tender fish and a peppercorn crust.

**1** Lay the four monkfish fillets flat on a board. Cut two slices from each of the citrus fruits and spread them on top of two of the fillets.

**2** Add a few sprigs of thyme and sprinkle the fish with salt and pepper. Finely grate the rind from the remaining fruit and sprinkle it over the fish.

**3** Cover each topped fillet with a plain fillet, cut side down, and tie firmly at intervals with fine cotton string to hold the stuffing in place. Place in a dish.

**4** Squeeze the juice from all the citrus fruits and mix with the olive oil. Add a little salt and pepper and spoon the mixture over the fish. Cover and marinate for 30 minutes, turning occasionally.

**5** Drain the monkfish, reserving the marinade, and sprinkle with the crushed peppercorns. Grill on a barbecue or hot griddle over a medium heat for about 15–20 minutes, turning occasionally and basting with the marinade, until the monkfish is evenly cooked. Remove the string and serve immediately.

## INGREDIENTS

SERVES 4

2 monkfish tails, each about
   350g/12oz, filleted into four
1 lime
1 lemon
2 oranges
30ml/2 tbsp olive oil
handful of fresh thyme sprigs
15ml/1 tbsp mixed peppercorns,
   roughly crushed
salt and ground black pepper

# SPICY BEEF SALAD WITH SWEET POTATO

The beef and sweet potatoes are cooked ahead, so there's no last-minute panic, making this a perfect dish for entertaining, or when it's difficult to be in complete control of timing.

## INGREDIENTS

SERVES 6

800g/1¾lb fillet of beef, in
  the piece
5ml/1 tsp black peppercorns,
  crushed
10ml/2 tsp chopped fresh thyme
60ml/4 tbsp olive oil
45ml/3 tbsp white wine
2 garlic cloves, crushed
450g/1lb orange-fleshed
  sweet potatoes
salt and ground black pepper

FOR THE DRESSING

1 garlic clove, chopped
60ml/4 tbsp chopped fresh flat
  leaf parsley
30ml/2 tbsp chopped fresh
  coriander (cilantro)
15ml/1 tbsp small salted
  capers, rinsed
1 fresh green chilli, seeded
  and chopped
10ml/2 tsp Dijon mustard
10–15ml/2–3 tsp white
  wine vinegar
75ml/5 tbsp extra virgin olive oil
2 shallots, finely chopped

**1** Roll the beef fillet in the crushed peppercorns and thyme, then place it in a shallow non-metallic dish. Mix 30ml/2 tbsp of the oil with the wine and garlic, pour the mixture over the meat, cover and marinate for 2–3 hours.

**2** Drain the beef. Sear on all sides on an oiled barbecue grill over a high heat, then move to a cooler part of the barbecue and cook for 20–30 minutes or until cooked to your taste. Remove from the heat, wrap in foil and set aside.

**3** Peel the sweet potatoes and cut them lengthways into 1cm/½in slices. Brush with the remaining olive oil, season with salt and pepper and cook on a griddle on the hob or barbecue over a medium heat for 5–6 minutes on each side, until tender and browned. Cut into strips and place in a bowl.

**4** Make the dressing by processing the garlic, parsley, coriander, capers, chilli, mustard and 10ml/2 tsp of the vinegar in a food processor or blender until the herbs are finely chopped. With the motor

running, slowly pour in the oil. Season with salt and pepper, taste and add more vinegar if needed. Stir in the shallots.

**5** Cut the beef into strips and add to the sweet potatoes. Pour over the dressing, toss lightly and leave to stand for up to 2 hours before serving.

### COOK'S TIP

If you prefer to cook the meat on a griddle, cut the fillet into steaks first. Depending on their thickness and whether you like them rare or well cooked, they will take 2–4 minutes on each side.

# KOREAN MARINATED BEEF STEAKS

These thin steaks take only seconds to cook, and work best on a griddle or barbecue wok.

## INGREDIENTS

SERVES 3–4

450g/1lb rump steak, in the piece
sesame oil, for frying
4 spring onions (scallions)
2.5cm/1in piece fresh root ginger
150ml/¹/₄ pint/²/₃ cup dark
    soy sauce
30ml/2 tbsp sesame oil
30ml/2 tbsp sake or dry
    white wine
2 garlic cloves, cut into thin slivers
15ml/1 tbsp sugar
15ml/1 tbsp sesame seeds

**1** Put the meat into the freezer until it is firm enough to slice very thinly and evenly. Put the slices of beef in a dish.

**2** Cut the spring onions into 2.5cm/1in lengths. Peel and finely chop the ginger. Make the marinade by mixing the soy sauce and oil with the sake or wine in a bowl. Add the garlic, sugar, ginger, sesame seeds and spring onion pieces.

**3** Pour the marinade over the beef. Cover the dish and marinate in the refrigerator for 4–6 hours, or preferably overnight.

**4** Heat the merest slick of oil in a griddle or a barbecue wok over a high heat. Remove the beef slices from the marinade, dry on kitchen paper, and fry for a few seconds, turning once.

**5** Pour the marinade on to the beef, and allow it to sizzle for a few seconds to heat through. Remove from the heat and serve immediately..

# CHILLI BURGERS WITH TORTILLAS AND GUACAMOLE

These burgers are absolutely delicious. The guacamole is an instant soother for the fiery chilli.

**1** Mix the minced steak with the chilli, onion, green pepper and garlic. Add the Tabasco and mix well with clean hands. Shape into four large, round burgers.

**2** Brush the burgers with oil and cook on a hot griddle or on a barbecue over a medium heat for 8–10 minutes, turning once, until golden brown.

**3** When the burgers are almost ready, heat the tortillas quickly in the microwave, under a hot grill (broiler) or on the barbecue. Place a burger and a generous spoonful of guacamole on one half of each tortilla and flip the clear side over to partly cover. Garnish with coriander and serve with dressed lettuce leaves.

**COOK'S TIP**
If you want to make your own guacamole, mash 2 ripe avocados and mix with 1 crushed garlic clove, 2 chopped tomatoes, 30ml/2 tbsp chopped fresh coriander (cilantro) and the juice of 1 lime.

**INGREDIENTS**

SERVES 4

500g/1¼lb lean minced (ground) steak
1 green chilli, finely chopped
1 small onion, finely chopped
1 small green (bell) pepper, finely chopped
1 garlic clove, crushed
generous dash of Tabasco sauce
oil, for brushing
4 fresh tortillas
guacamole and dressed lettuce leaves, to serve
chopped fresh coriander (cilantro), to garnish

# GREEK LAMB KEBABS

The secret of these souvlakia, as they are known in their native Greece, is to have large chunks of top quality lamb with a little fat to keep them moist during cooking.

**1** Put the oil, lemon juice, garlic and herbs in a large bowl. Season with salt and pepper and whisk well to combine. Add the meat cubes, stirring to coat them in the mixture. Cover and marinate in the refrigerator for 4–8 hours, stirring several times.

**2** Separate the onion quarters into pieces, each composed of two or three layers, and slice each pepper quarter in half widthways.

**3** Lift out the meat cubes from the marinade, and thread them on long metal skewers, alternating each piece of meat with a piece of pepper and onion.

**4** Brush the lamb and vegetables with the marinade and cook them on a barbecue or griddle over a medium to high heat for 10 minutes, until they start to scorch slightly. Brush with marinade, turn them over, brush once more and cook for a further 10–15 minutes. Serve straight away.

## INGREDIENTS

SERVES 4

75ml/5 tbsp extra virgin olive oil
juice of 1 lemon
2 garlic cloves, crushed
2.5ml/$^1$/$_2$ tsp dried oregano
2.5ml/$^1$/$_2$ tsp dried thyme,
    or 5ml/1 tsp fresh thyme
    leaves, chopped
1 small shoulder of lamb, boned,
    trimmed and cut into
    4cm/1$^1$/$_2$in cubes
2–3 red onions, quartered
2 red or green (bell) peppers,
    quartered and seeded
salt and ground black pepper

# MINTED LAMB PATTIES WITH REDCURRANT CHUTNEY

The cubes of mozzarella hidden in these lamb patties give them a lovely texture. For colour, and to counter the richness, they are served with redcurrant and mint chutney.

## INGREDIENTS

SERVES 4

500g/1¼lb minced (ground) lean lamb
1 shallot, finely chopped
30ml/2 tbsp finely chopped fresh mint
30ml/2 tbsp finely chopped fresh parsley
115g/4oz mozzarella cheese
salt and ground black pepper
oil, for brushing

FOR THE CHUTNEY

175g/6oz/1½ cups fresh or thawed frozen redcurrants
10ml/2 tsp clear honey
5ml/1 tsp balsamic vinegar
30ml/2 tbsp finely chopped fresh mint

### COOK'S TIP

If you like, serve the patties in burger buns or with crusty bread, along with a mixed leaf salad.

**1** Mix the lamb, shallot, mint and parsley in a bowl. The easiest way to do this is with clean hands. Season with plenty of salt and pepper.

**2** Divide the mixture into eight equal pieces and shape each into a flat round.

**3** Cut the mozzarella into four cubes. Sandwich the rounds together in pairs, with a cube of mozzarella in the centre. Press together firmly, making sure that the cheese is completely sealed inside each patty.

**4** Make the chutney by mixing the redcurrants, honey, vinegar and mint in a bowl. Season with salt and pepper, then mash with a fork so that some of the redcurrant juices are released.

**5** Brush the lamb patties with oil and cook them on the barbecue or a griddle over a medium to high heat, turning once, for about 15 minutes or until they are golden brown and cooked through. Serve with the redcurrant chutney.

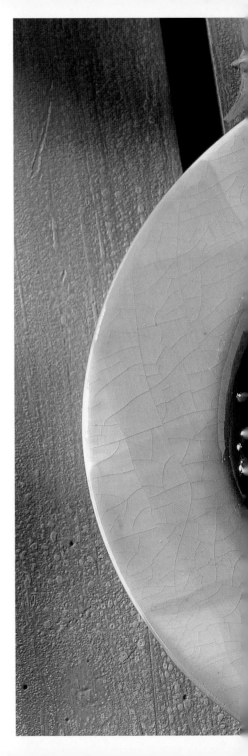

# THAI-SPICED PORK CHOPS WITH MUSHROOMS

Both pork and mushrooms taste great with this Thai-style marinade. The sauce, and the noodles, need to be briefly cooked in a pan, so if you are outdoors a quick retreat to the kitchen might be needed.

**1** Make the marinade by mixing all the ingredients in a shallow dish which is large enough to hold all the pork chops in a single layer.

**2** Add the pork chops, turning to coat well. Cover and marinate for 1–2 hours.

**3** Lift the chops out of the marinade and place on a barbecue over a medium heat or on a hot griddle. Cook for 5–7 minutes, until browned.

**4** Turn the pork chops over. Brush the mushrooms with the oil and place them next to the pork chops.

**5** Brush both with the marinade and cook for 5–7 minutes more, moving the mushrooms to a cooler part of the grill after 2–3 minutes. Make sure the pork chops are completely cooked through.

**6** To make the sauce, heat a little oil in a wok or frying pan and stir-fry the red chillies with the shallots for 1–2 minutes. Stir in the Thai fish sauce, lime juice, ground rice and chopped spring onions. Heat through, then pour over the pork chops.

**7** Garnish with the shredded spring onions and serve with noodles.

## INGREDIENTS

SERVES 4

4 pork chops
4 large field (portabello) mushrooms
45ml/3 tbsp vegetable oil
4 fresh red chillies, seeded and thinly sliced
4 shallots, chopped
45ml/3 tbsp Thai fish sauce
15ml/1 tbsp fresh lime juice
5ml/1 tsp roasted ground rice
30ml/2 tbsp chopped spring onions (scallions), plus extra, shredded, to garnish
noodles, to serve

FOR THE MARINADE

2 garlic cloves, crushed
15ml/1 tbsp sugar
15ml/1 tbsp Thai fish sauce
30ml/2 tbsp soy sauce
15ml/1 tbsp sesame oil
15ml/1 tbsp whisky or dry sherry
2 lemon grass stalks, finely chopped
2 spring onions (scallions), chopped

# PORK AND PINEAPPLE SATAY

For sheer flavour and ease of eating, there's nothing to beat these Indonesian pork and pineapple skewers, served in the traditional style with a coconut milk and peanut sauce.

## INGREDIENTS

SERVES 4

1 small onion, chopped
1 garlic clove, crushed
60ml/4 tbsp soy sauce
finely grated rind of 1/2 lemon
5ml/1 tsp ground cumin
5ml/1 tsp ground coriander
5ml/1 tsp ground turmeric
5ml/1 tsp soft dark brown sugar
1 small pineapple, peeled
    and diced
500g/11/4lb pork fillet (tenderloin)

FOR THE SAUCE

175ml/6fl oz/3/4 cup
    coconut milk
90ml/6 tbsp crunchy
    peanut butter
1 garlic clove, crushed
10ml/2 tsp soy sauce
5ml/1 tsp soft dark brown sugar

**1** Place the onion, garlic, soy sauce, lemon rind, spices and sugar in a blender or food processor. Add 2 pieces of pineapple and process until the mixture is almost smooth.

**2** Trim any fat from the pork fillet and cut the meat into 2.5cm/1in cubes. Place in a large bowl, add the spiced pineapple mixture and toss well to coat evenly. Leave to marinate for an hour.

**3** Thread the pork cubes on soaked bamboo or metal skewers, alternating each cube of spiced meat with a piece of pineapple.

**4** Make the sauce. Pour the coconut milk into a small pan and add the peanut butter. Mix well, then stir in the crushed garlic, soy sauce and brown sugar. Heat gently on the hob or over the barbecue, stirring until smooth and hot. Cover and keep warm.

**5** Cook the pork and pineapple skewers over a medium heat on the barbecue or on a griddle for 10–12 minutes, turning occasionally, until golden brown and completely cooked. Serve with the warm satay sauce.

### COOK'S TIP

This works best if you cook the kebabs on the barbecue or under a conventional grill (broiler). If you use a griddle, use metal skewers and turn them frequently. Test the pork to make quite sure it is cooked through before serving.

# CHARGRILLED CHICKEN WITH GARLIC AND PEPPERS

Marinated chicken is a great choice for the barbecue or grill. Cooking the pepper skewers and tomatoes separately works well and they make a great accompaniment.

## INGREDIENTS

SERVES 4

12 chicken thighs, with skin
1 red (bell) pepper, quartered
    and seeded
1 green (bell) pepper, quartered
    and seeded
4 tomatoes, halved horizontally
lemon wedges, to serve

FOR THE MARINADE

90ml/6 tbsp extra virgin olive oil
juice of 1 large lemon
5ml/1 tsp Dijon mustard
4 garlic cloves, crushed
4 fresh red or green chillies,
    seeded and chopped
5ml/1 tsp dried oregano
salt and ground black pepper

**1** Beat all the marinade ingredients together in a large bowl. Make a couple of slits in the thickest parts of the chicken pieces so that the marinade will penetrate deeply and the chicken will cook more quickly.

**2** Add the chicken pieces to the marinade and turn them over to coat them thoroughly. Cover the bowl and place in the refrigerator for 4–8 hours, turning the chicken pieces several times.

**3** About 15 minutes before starting to cook, lift the chicken pieces out of the marinade and set them aside on a plate.

Add the pepper pieces and halved tomatoes to the marinade and set aside.

**4** Grill the chicken pieces for about 20 minutes on each side over medium heat on a barbecue or for slightly less time on a griddle.

**5** Meanwhile, drain the vegetables and thread the peppers on four metal skewers. Grill them, with the tomatoes, alongside the chicken for about 15 minutes.

**6** Check that the chicken is cooked through. Serve with the pepper skewers, grilled tomatoes and lemon wedges.

### COOK'S TIP

If cooking on a barbecue, wait until the first flush of heat has begun to subside. Watch the chicken pieces carefully and move them to a cooler area if they start to scorch.

# MINI CHICKEN KEBABS WITH DIPPING SAUCE

Serve these delicious miniature kebabs as party snacks, or as a first course at a barbecue.

## INGREDIENTS

SERVES 4

4 skinless, boneless chicken
   breast portions
2 garlic cloves, crushed
2.5cm/1in piece fresh root
   ginger, finely grated
10ml/2 tsp Thai fish sauce
30ml/2 tbsp light soy sauce
15ml/1 tbsp clear honey
spring onion (scallion) green,
   to garnish

FOR THE DIPPING SAUCE

105ml/7 tbsp light soy sauce
15ml/1 tbsp sweet chilli sauce

**1** Soak 16 wooden satay sticks or kebab skewers in water for 30 minutes to prevent them from scorching during cooking. Make the dipping sauce by mixing the ingredients in a jug (pitcher). Divide among four small dishes.

**2** Slice each chicken breast into four long strips. Mix the garlic, ginger, fish sauce, soy sauce and honey in a large bowl, add the chicken strips and toss to coat. Cover and marinate in the refrigerator for at least 30 minutes, or overnight.

**3** Drain the chicken strips and thread each one on a drained wooden skewer. Cook over medium heat on the barbecue or griddle for 3–5 minutes, until the chicken is golden brown and completely cooked through.

**4** Garnish the skewers with spring onion green and serve with the individual bowls of dipping sauce.

# POUSSINS WITH LIME AND CHILLIES

These spatchcocked little chickens are best cooked on the barbecue.

**1** All the poussins are prepared in the same way. Place a bird breast upwards on a board and press down firmly with a clean hand to break the breastbone, then turn the bird over and cut down either side of the backbone so that you can remove it.

**2** Turn the bird breast up again and flatten it. Lift the breast skin carefully and gently ease it away from the flesh.

**3** Mix the butter, tomato purée, lime rind and chilli sauce. Using three-quarters of the mixture, spread some under the skin of each bird. Smooth the skin back over. Thread two skewers crosswise through each bird to hold it securely.

**4** Mix the remaining paste with the lime juice and brush it over the birds. Cook over a medium to high heat on a barbecue or griddle, turning once or twice, until the chicken is cooked through. Serve garnished with flat leaf parsley and lime wedges.

## INGREDIENTS

SERVES 4

4 poussins or Cornish hens, each about 450g/1lb
45ml/3 tbsp softened butter
30ml/2 tbsp sun-dried tomato purée (paste)
finely grated rind of 1 lime
10ml/2 tsp chilli sauce
juice of 1 lime
flat leaf parsley sprigs and lime wedges, to garnish

# GRILLED PHEASANTS WITH SAGE

Although these could be cooked on a griddle, their size makes it
more practical to use a barbecue grill. Tucking the sage mixture
under the skin gives the birds a delicious flavour.

**INGREDIENTS**

SERVES 4

2 pheasants, each
   about 450g/1lb
1 lemon
60ml/4 tbsp chopped fresh
   sage leaves
3 shallots
5ml/1 tsp Dijon mustard
15ml/1 tbsp brandy
150ml/¼ pint/⅔ cup
   crème fraîche
salt and ground black pepper
lemon wedges and sage sprigs,
   to garnish

**1** Place the pheasants, breast side
upwards, on a board, and cut them in
half lengthways, using poultry shears or a
sharp knife.

**2** Finely grate the rind from half the
lemon and slice the rest thinly. Mix the
grated rind with half the chopped sage
in a bowl.

**3** Loosen the skin on the breast and legs
of each of the pheasants and insert a
little of the sage mixture under it. Tuck the
lemon slices under the skin and smooth
the skin back firmly.

**4** Cook each half pheasant over a
medium heat on a barbecue or griddle for
30 minutes, until thoroughly cooked,
turning once.

**5** Meanwhile, place the unpeeled shallots
on the barbecue or griddle and cook for
10–12 minutes, turning occasionally, until
the skin has blackened and the centres
are very soft.

**6** Peel off the shallot skins, chop the flesh
roughly and place in a bowl. Mash it with
the mustard and brandy, stir in the crème
fraîche and add the reserved chopped
sage and salt and pepper to taste.

**7** Garnish the pheasants with lemon
wedges and sprigs of sage and serve
with the shallot sauce.

# POTATO SKEWERS WITH MUSTARD DIP

Caramelized shallots and grilled new potatoes taste wonderful with a mustard mayonnaise.

## INGREDIENTS

SERVES 4

4 garlic cloves, crushed
2 egg yolks
30ml/2 tbsp lemon juice
300ml/$\frac{1}{2}$ pint/1$\frac{1}{4}$ cups olive oil,
    plus extra for brushing
10ml/2 tsp wholegrain mustard
1kg/2$\frac{1}{4}$lb small new potatoes
200g/7oz shallots, peeled
    and halved
15ml/1 tbsp sea salt
salt and ground black pepper

**1** Make the dip. Mix the garlic, egg yolks and lemon juice in a blender or food processor. Process for a few seconds until the mixture is smooth.

**2** Have the oil ready in a jug (pitcher). With the motor running, add the oil very gradually, pouring it in a slow, steady stream through the aperture in the lid. When the mixture is smooth and glossy, add the mustard, whiz briefly, then scrape the mixture into a bowl. Stir in salt and pepper to taste.

**3** Bring a pan of water to the boil, add the potatoes and cook for 5 minutes. Drain well, then thread on to metal skewers, alternately with the shallots.

**4** Brush the skewers with oil and sprinkle with the sea salt. Cook over a medium heat on a barbecue or griddle for 10–12 minutes, turning occasionally, until the potatoes are cooked through. Serve while warm, with the dip.

# MEDITERRANEAN VEGETABLES WITH PESTO SWIRL

A cool yogurt and pesto sauce makes the perfect accompaniment to grilled vegetables.

**1** Cut the aubergines into 1cm/¹/₂in thick slices and halve the courgettes lengthways. Cut the peppers in half, through the stalks, and scrape out the pith and seeds. Slice the fennel and onion into thick wedges.

**2** Spoon the yogurt into a bowl and stir in the pesto lightly to make a swirly, marbled mixture. Set aside.

**3** Brush the vegetables with oil and cook them over a medium heat on a barbecue or griddle until golden brown and tender.

Sprinkle with salt and pepper after the first 2–3 minutes and press down with a spatula from time to time so that the surface of each vegetable becomes scored with marks from the grill or griddle. Serve with the pesto sauce.

**COOK'S TIP**

As each vegetable cooks, take it off the griddle or move it to a cooler part of the barbecue. The aubergines and peppers will take 6–8 minutes, the courgettes, onion and fennel 4–5 minutes.

**INGREDIENTS**

SERVES 4

2 small aubergines (eggplant)
2 large courgettes (zucchini)
1 red (bell) pepper
1 yellow (bell) pepper
1 fennel bulb
1 red onion
olive oil, for brushing
salt and ground black pepper

FOR THE SAUCE

150ml/¹/₄ pint/²/₃ cup Greek (US strained plain) yogurt
45ml/3 tbsp pesto

# RED BEAN AND MUSHROOM BURGERS

Bought veggie burgers are often grey and uninteresting, a far cry from these gourmet treats.

## INGREDIENTS

SERVES 4

15ml/1 tbsp olive oil
1 small onion, finely chopped
1 garlic clove, crushed
5ml/1 tsp ground cumin
5ml/1 tsp ground coriander
115g/4oz/1 cup mushrooms,
  finely chopped
400g/14oz can red kidney
  beans, drained
30ml/2 tbsp chopped fresh
  coriander (cilantro)
salt and ground black pepper
flour, for shaping
pitta bread and salad, to serve

**1** Heat the oil in a wide pan and fry the onion and garlic for 3 minutes, until softened. Add the spices and cook for 1 minute more, stirring constantly.

**2** Add the mushrooms and cook, stirring, until all the liquid has evaporated. Remove from the heat.

**3** Mash the drained red kidney beans with a fork and stir them into the mushroom mixture. Add the fresh coriander and salt and pepper to taste. Mix well.

**4** Using floured hands, shape the mixture into four flat patties. If the mixture is too sticky to handle, mix in a little flour.

**5** Brush the burgers with oil and cook for 8–10 minutes over a medium to high heat on a barbecue or griddle, turning once. Serve with pitta bread and a salad.

### COOK'S TIP
A bowl of Greek (US strained plain) yogurt, with pieces of chopped cucumber and crushed garlic stirred in, goes well with the burgers.

# COURGETTE AND GOAT'S CHEESE SPLITS

The perfect choice for a warm summer's evening.

**1** Trim the stem end of each courgette. Bring a shallow pan of water to the boil, add the courgettes and cook over a low heat for 6–8 minutes, until just beginning to soften. Drain and set aside until cold.

**2** Cut a deep slit in the side of each courgette. Gently ease the slits apart and insert a couple of strips of goat's cheese in each courgette. Add a little mint and sprinkle with pepper.

**3** Brush the courgettes with olive oil, and cook on a hot griddle for 4–5 minutes,

moving them frequently so that the skin becomes lightly browned and the cheese melts. Do not turn them over completely, or you will lose the filling, but use the grooves on the griddle to support them as you brown the sides. Do not let the skin burn or it will become bitter.

**4** To bake on the barbecue, place the filled courgettes, filling side up, in a hinged barbecue and cook over a medium heat, without turning, or wrap the courgettes in foil and cook on the barbecue grill for 15–20 minutes.

### INGREDIENTS

SERVES 4

8 small courgettes (zucchini)
75–115g/3–4oz goat's cheese
    cut into thin strips
small bunch fresh mint,
    finely chopped
15ml/1 tbsp extra virgin olive oil
ground black pepper

# AUBERGINE SLICES WITH RICH TOMATO TOPPING

When your dinner guests include vegetarians, this is the perfect dish. Everyone will enjoy the robust flavours and it can be cooked before any meat is placed on the grill.

## INGREDIENTS

SERVES 4

150ml/¼ pint/⅔ cup extra virgin olive oil
2 large onions, finely chopped
3 garlic cloves, finely chopped
500g/1¼lb tomatoes, chopped
2.5ml/½ tsp dried oregano
2.5ml/½ tsp dried thyme
2.5ml/½ tsp sugar
15ml/1 tbsp tomato purée (paste)
3 aubergines (eggplant), total weight about 800g/1¾lb
45ml/3 tbsp chopped fresh parsley
salt and ground black pepper

**1** Heat half the oil in a heavy pan and fry the onions for about 5 minutes over a low heat until tender and lightly coloured. Add the garlic and tomatoes. Stir in the oregano, thyme, sugar and tomato purée, cover the pan and cook for 15 minutes, stirring occasionally.

**2** Trim the aubergines and cut them into 1cm/½in thick rounds. Brush the remaining olive oil over the aubergine slices to coat them generously.

**3** Cook the aubergine slices on a hot griddle or over a medium heat on the barbecue for 10–15 minutes, turning once, until they are cooked through. Press them down lightly once or twice so that they acquire the stripes typical of griddled or grilled food. Place the cooked aubergine slices in a single layer in a shallow dish.

**4** Season the tomato sauce with salt and pepper and stir in the parsley. Pile a little of the mixture on each aubergine round. Serve warm.

# ROASTED RED ONIONS WITH CRUMBLY CHEESE

Red onions acquire the most delectable sweet flavour when roasted on a barbecue.

## INGREDIENTS

SERVES 6

6 red onions of similar
   size, unpeeled
30ml/2 tbsp sun-dried tomato
   oil, olive oil or chilli oil
175g/6oz crumbly cheese, such
   as Lancashire, Caerphilly or
   Cheshire, roughly crumbled
a few chopped chives
ground black pepper

FOR THE FLAVOURED BUTTER

115g/4oz/½ cup butter, softened
6 drained sun-dried tomatoes in
   oil, finely chopped
30ml/2 tbsp chopped fresh basil
   or parsley

**1** Tidy the onions up by removing any discoloured or torn layers of skin. Stand each onion, stem uppermost, on a board, and cut it almost but not quite into quarters so that it can be opened out.

**2** Place each onion on a square of heavy duty foil and drizzle a little of the oil into the centre. Wrap securely.

**3** Cook on a barbecue grill over a medium heat for 30–45 minutes, or until cooked through. When lightly squeezed with tongs, the onions will feel soft.

**4** While the onions are cooking, make the flavoured butter by beating the butter, chopped herbs, and chopped sun-dried tomatoes together in a bowl. Shape into a log, wrap in foil and chill.

**5** Carefully unwrap the onions and place them on a plate. Season with plenty of black pepper and add chunks of the sun-dried tomato butter to the central cavity. Sprinkle the cheese and chives over the top and eat immediately, mashing the soft, sweet onion flesh with the melting butter and cheese.

# GRIDDLED TOMATOES ON SODA BREAD

A perfect appetizer, the tomatoes are grilled until they begin to blacken, then piled on toast.

**1** Brush the tomato slices with olive oil. Cook on a hot griddle on the hob or barbecue for about 4 minutes, turning once, until softened and slightly blackened.

**2** Toast the soda bread until pale golden. If you are cooking the tomato slices on the barbecue, toast the bread on the barbecue grill.

**3** Place three or four tomato slices on each piece of toast and drizzle with olive oil and balsamic vinegar. Season with salt and pepper and serve immediately, with thin shavings of Parmesan.

### VARIATIONS
• Top the toast with prosciutto before adding the tomatoes.
• Use goat's cheese instead of Parmesan.
• Add extra flavour with anchovies or capers, or torn fresh basil leaves.

### INGREDIENTS
SERVES 4

6 tomatoes, thickly sliced
olive oil, for brushing
    and drizzling
4 thick slices soda bread
balsamic vinegar, for drizzling
salt and ground black pepper
shavings of Parmesan cheese,
    to serve

# GRIDDLED GREEK CHEESE WITH ROCKET

The rich, salty flavour of Halloumi cheese goes well with peppery rocket and lemon juice.

**INGREDIENTS**

SERVES 4

30ml/2 tbsp olive oil
8 slices Halloumi or Kefalotyri
   cheese, about 1cm/$^1$/$_2$in thick
ground black pepper
lemon wedges, to serve

FOR THE SALAD

15ml/1 tbsp red wine vinegar
60ml/4 tbsp extra virgin olive oil
a large handful of rocket
   (arugula) leaves

**1** Make a dressing for the salad by whisking the vinegar and olive oil in a bowl. Add the rocket leaves and toss until lightly coated. Divide among four salad plates.

**2** Heat a large griddle, either on the hob or on a barbecue over a medium heat. Pour the olive oil into a shallow bowl and dip in the slices of cheese to coat them evenly.

**3** Using tongs, transfer the pieces of cheese to the griddle. Do not let them

touch, or they will be difficult to separate. Let them sizzle for 2–3 minutes, turning once when crisp at the sides.

**4** Sprinkle the griddled cheese slices with pepper. As soon as the undersides turn golden, remove them from the pan and arrange on the dressed rocket. Serve immediately, with the lemon wedges for squeezing over the top.

# GRILLED LEEK AND FENNEL SALAD

This salad, with its piquant flavours, would go very well with any kind of grilled fish.

**1** Cook the leeks in boiling salted water for 4–5 minutes. Lift out with a slotted spoon. Keep the cooking water in the pan. When the leeks are cool, squeeze out the excess water, and cut them into short lengths.

**2** Trim the fennel and cut into wedges. Cook in the water used for the leeks for 5 minutes, drain, and toss with 30ml/ 2 tbsp of the olive oil. Season with pepper.

**3** Heat a griddle, either on the hob or on the barbecue. Add the leeks and fennel

and cook until tinged with brown, turning once. Transfer to a dish and set aside.

**4** Place the remaining olive oil in a heavy pan and add the shallots, wine, fennel seeds, herbs and chilli flakes. Bring to the boil, then simmer for 10 minutes. Add the tomatoes and cook for 8 minutes, until reduced. Season with salt and pepper.

**5** Pour the dressing over the leeks and fennel, toss to mix and leave to cool. Serve at room temperature.

## INGREDIENTS

SERVES 4–6

675g/1¹/₂lb leeks, trimmed
2 large fennel bulbs
120ml/4fl oz/¹/₂ cup olive oil
2 shallots, chopped
150ml/¹/₄ pint/²/₃ cup white wine
5ml/1 tsp fennel seeds, crushed
6 fresh thyme sprigs
2–3 bay leaves
pinch of dried red chilli flakes
350g/12oz tomatoes, peeled,
    seeded and diced
salt and ground black pepper

# BAKED BANANAS WITH VANILLA ICE

The easiest dessert imaginable. The fruit becomes meltingly soft and is delicious with ice cream.

## INGREDIENTS

SERVES 4

4 large bananas
4 large scoops of vanilla
    ice cream

FOR THE SAUCE

25g/1oz/2 tbsp unsalted
    (sweet) butter
50g/2oz/¹/₂ cup hazelnuts,
    toasted and roughly chopped
45ml/3 tbsp golden
    (light corn) syrup
30ml/2 tbsp lemon juice

**1** Place the bananas in their skins on the barbecue grill over a medium heat. Leave for about 10 minutes or until the skins are uniformly black and the flesh gives a little when the bananas are gently squeezed.

**2** Meanwhile, make the sauce. Melt the butter in a small pan. Add the nuts and cook gently for 1 minute. Stir in the syrup and lemon juice and heat, stirring, for 1 minute more.

**3** To serve, slit each banana open and ease the skin apart to reveal the cooked fruit. Place on serving plates and serve with the ice cream and hot sauce.

### COOK'S TIP

The timing for cooking the bananas isn't critical. If you've cooked the rest of the meal on the barbecue, just pop the bananas on to the grill when you take the last main course item off. The sauce can be made ahead of time and kept warm at the side of the grill.

# MANGO AND PINEAPPLE ON TOASTED PANETTONE

Cooking tropical fruit on the grill concentrates its sweetness, and gives it a caramel flavour.

**1** To prepare the mango, cut off the thick portions, or cheeks, on either side of the stone (pit). Remove the skin and slice the flesh in wedges. Cut off the remaining flesh from the stone, peel and cut it into neat pieces.

**2** Cut the top and the bottom off the pineapple with a large sharp knife, and slice off the skin, removing as many of the "eyes" as possible. Cut the pineapple lengthways into quarters. Cut out the core from each quarter, then slice the pineapple into thick wedges.

**3** Heat a griddle on the hob or the barbecue. Add the fruit, in batches if necessary, and brush it all over with the melted butter. Cook for 8 minutes, turning once, until soft and slightly golden.

**4** Meanwhile, spoon the yogurt into a bowl and stir in the honey, cinnamon and vanilla essence.

**5** Toast the panettone lightly, place one slice on each plate and top with the griddled pineapple and mango. Serve with the vanilla yogurt.

**INGREDIENTS**

SERVES 4

1 large mango
1 large pineapple
25g/1oz/2 tbsp unsalted (sweet) butter, melted
4 thick slices panettone

FOR THE VANILLA YOGURT

250g/9oz/generous 1 cup Greek (US strained plain) yogurt
30ml/2 tbsp clear honey
2.5ml/$\frac{1}{2}$ tsp ground cinnamon
a few drops of vanilla essence (extract)

# NECTARINES WITH MARZIPAN AND MASCARPONE

*After a delicious al fresco meal, the last thing you want to do is a complicated dessert.*

**INGREDIENTS**

SERVES 4

4 firm, ripe nectarines
75g/3oz marzipan
75g/3oz/6 tbsp mascarpone
  cheese
3 ratafia biscuits (almond
  macaroons), crushed

**1** Using a sharp knife, cut the nectarines in half and remove the stones (pits).

**2** Cut the marzipan into eight pieces and press one piece into the stone cavity in each nectarine half.

**3** Spoon the mascarpone on top, hiding the marzipan completely. Sprinkle over the crushed ratafia biscuits.

**4** Place the half fruits on a hot barbecue or griddle for 3–5 minutes, until they are hot and the mascarpone begins to melt. Serve immediately.

**VARIATION**

You can also use peaches for this recipe.

# GLAZED PINEAPPLE WITH RUM BUTTER

The rum glaze gives the pineapples a lovely golden colour, and they taste superb.

**1** With a sharp cook's knife, divide the pineapple lengthways into quarters, cutting right through the leafy green top. Cut away the hard core from each piece of pineapple.

**2** Cut between the pineapple flesh and skin to release the flesh, but do not lift off the fruit. Slice the flesh across in chunks.

**3** Push a bamboo skewer lengthways through each chunk and into the leafy stalk, to hold them in place along the length of the pineapple wedge.

**4** Mix the sugar, ginger, melted butter and rum in a bowl. Brush the mixture over the pineapple. Cook the wedges on a hot barbecue for 3–4 minutes, then transfer each glazed pineapple "boat" to a serving plate. Pour over any remaining glaze and serve.

**INGREDIENTS**

SERVES 4

1 medium pineapple, with
   leafy crown
30ml/2 tbsp soft dark
   brown sugar
5ml/1 tsp ground ginger
50g/2oz/¼ cup unsalted (sweet)
   butter, melted
30ml/2 tbsp dark rum

# INDEX